Table of Contents

Chapter 1: 3
   Introduction 3

Chapter 2: 5
   Random Thoughts, Tips, and Theory 5

Chapter 3: 9
   Meal Planning: How to Eat Like it's on Purpose 9

Chapter 4: 14
   Emergency Meal Planning 14

Chapter 5: 16
   Grocery Shopping: More Fun than Shoe Shopping (if you're me) 16

Chapter 6: 22
   Prepping and Freezer Meals 22

Chapter 7: 28
   Recipes and Techniques 28
      Pasta 28
      Fried Things 28
      Potato Chips 29
      Appetizers, Breads, and Side Dishes 29
      Dressings 34
      Entrees 34
      Chicken 34
      Pasta 38
      Vegetarian 40
      Beef and Other 43
      Salmon 48
      Desserts 49

Chapter 8: 51
   Non-Food Saving Tips: Where to Find Money! 51

Chapter 9: 55
   Impress on a Dime 55

Chapter 10: 58
   Breastfeeding – Oh, What's Milk Got to Do, Got to Do with It? 58

Chapter 11: 60
   The Exciting Conclusion 60

Index of Recipes 61

EATING ON THE CHEAP
BY KOLBI WARD

Chapter 1:

Introduction

I know we are all just doing our best in this crazy world we live in. I trust you do a great job feeding your family, but a few new ideas are always helpful – knowledge is power and all that jazz. This is not an extensive cookbook; it's more of a walk-through of what we actually eat day to day. It is organized in much the same way my brain is organized – not much at all. You will get to know my personality a bit as we go; I am a bit ditzy, usually perky, uber practical, and overtly cheap (also, lazy and snarky, I could go on, but I won't).

So, who am I? Let's hit the highlights:

Photo by Kathryn Fishman-Weaver

My name is Kolbi Ward and I am an at-home mom of three kids. I am also the director of a food pantry where we distribute all the ingredients for full meals along with the recipes to make at least six meals, each under $5. Those recipes came from this book with only a few minor changes to make them easier to prepare.

Levi is 18 and attends public school as a senior (he was homeschooled until sophomore year). He is a fantastic young man – responsible and polite. He loves babies and young children, but is frequently annoyed by his teen sister. His passions are psychology and history.

Paige is 13 and is homeschooled. She is vibrant and spunky. She loves Pinterest, cooking, her pet rats, and being a great assistant with her baby sister. She doesn't like working on her school, but other than that, is quite pleasant. I love when she comes downstairs with her new craft creations, she is always so proud!

3

Lucille is 2 and is energetic and adorable. Her favorite things are nursing, daddy, and the big kids. Daddy calls her Goose. She loves to dance and has an inexplicably strong affection for reggae.

I married Doug Ward on October 1, 2011 after several years of dating. He is a wonderful husband, step-father, and father. He has a curious and dry sense of humor and a cranky façade, but is truly a kind person who loves kids. He is the General Manager of a steakhouse.

We try to live and parent in a healthy, natural, gentle environment. We aren't perfect, but do our best.

I have a passion for nutrition, health, breastfeeding, and first aid and spend a fair amount of time keeping current on these topics. I have noticed that I frequently say things that seem like common sense to me, but are foreign to a lot of people, hence the compiling of this simple book. I know that 100 years ago, everything I do would have been taught in the home, but somehow we have gotten away from these basic concepts.

My goal for this little book is to offer some information that you may not know, remind you of things you may have forgotten, empower you to change and make rules that fit your family, and hopefully do all of that in a way that is friendly and at least mildly entertaining. Let's go!

Quotes I find entertaining:

I don't like food that's too carefully arranged; it makes me think that the chef is spending too much time arranging and not enough time cooking. If I wanted a picture I'd buy a painting.
-Andy Rooney

"Omit and substitute! That's how recipes should be written. Please don't ever get so hung up on published recipes that you forget that you can omit and substitute."
-Jeff Smith, The Frugal Gourmet

Once, during prohibition, I was forced to live for days on nothing but food and water.
-W.C. Fields

Chapter 2:

Random Thoughts, Tips, and Theory

I rarely spend more than 30 minutes making any meal. The only exception is when something takes longer than that in the oven, but still, my actual hands-on cooking time is less than 30 minutes, usually closer to 15. This in no way means we eat crap! I have worked in restaurants over half my life and one thing I have learned is that even the fanciest, most elaborate looking meal can be made in 15 minutes if you are properly prepped. If you treat your home kitchen like a tiny little restaurant, things are super fast! Plus, then you kind of feel like you have your own TV cooking show with a full staff of prep cooks when you make dinner! There are about five items that if you have prepped (diced and portioned) in the fridge or freezer at all times, you can make dinner with no chopping and only a few minutes of actual cooking. Ready? Big secret ahead – onions, peppers, carrots, celery, and cooked chicken. Add some homemade stock, some packaged frozen vegetables, perhaps some diced and sautéed sausage, bacon, or ham, some par-cooked beans, and maybe a salad and you are totally set. I just can not stress enough how vital prepping is to a lazy cook!

I almost always serve bread that is sliced, drizzled with olive oil, and put under the broiler with every meal. We love bread, it's a fact. This is also a super way to save a little money by using day old (or even several day old) bread.

We also eat some type of pasta and chicken nearly every day. I often think I should branch out but we all seem to be making it okay. By simply changing the seasonings you can make the same recipe taste totally different.

At least 80% of the things (other than breakfast and dessert) I cook contain garlic and I have a very firm "no garlic powder" rule. I think you should, too. It only takes a second to mince garlic in a garlic press or finely chop it and it tastes sooooo much better.

Pre-packaged meals are sub-standard and **you are worth** the few extra minutes it takes to make healthier, cheaper, tastier food. Plus, they are just plain unnecessary. If you have a well-stocked pantry, you can probably make any Hamburger Helper or Pasta Salad or canned soup type meal without opening a box or can.

I love my broiler; I use it all the time for bread, salmon, steaks, and bacon. Get to know your broiler; just remember to keep an eye on it!

A good cast-iron skillet is invaluable; it gets really hot and holds the temperature steady so things cook more evenly. Plus, you can put it right in the oven if you need to. My favorite place to find them is at antique or thrift stores. Some people are crazy about collecting certain names, but they are all great as far as I am concerned. I have a flat top glass cooktop so have to be relatively careful when choosing (and setting down and moving) my cast iron, but as long as it has a flat bottom (some have raised rings) then it is fine to use.

I have one teensy confession. I love pre-cooked bacon. I know how to make bacon (the easiest way is to just lay it out on a cookie sheet and bake at 400º for about 30 minutes) but I frequently burn it and I usually only need part of a package and it makes a splattery mess on the stove and the pre-cooked stuff it so easy… I know I'm rationalizing, but it really is a genius product. I usually get the store brand or name brand if it's on sale and I think that when you take into consideration the amount I burn, it's about the same price. I usually throw what I need in a skillet or under the broiler for a minute to crisp it or even the microwave sometimes. Is it as good as the real deal? Nope, but it is close enough for us most of the time.

I only have whole wheat flour on hand -A LOT of whole wheat flour- so anything that calls for flour gets that. It is healthier in lots of ways and just plain tastes better. After a while of only using whole wheat, white flour tastes like paste. There are some recipes that are heavier than if I had used white, but I don't think the difference is important enough to worry about finding recipes designed specifically for whole wheat. If you want to switch, you might start by doing half and half or so or buying "white whole wheat" which is a milder type of wheat.

I use my electric pressure cooker all the time. It is perfect for chicken, roast beef, and rice. It is a Toastmaster 4 Qt cooker. I don't think they actually make it anymore, but if you can find one used or another brand, I highly recommend it! Much bigger isn't practical unless you decide to take up canning (which is on my list to do, but I'm not organized enough just yet) and smaller won't fit a chicken or roast, which makes it worthless to me. It is the fastest and most fool proof way to get a whole chicken (35 minutes), a roast (about 20 minutes), and brown rice (18 minutes) perfectly done.

I also use my probe thermometer all the time. I am incredibly forgetful and easily distracted – shocking, I know! But it doesn't matter because I tell my friendly thermometer to remind me when the food is done. Just make sure you put it in the thickest part of the meat, not touching a bone and when it registers done, check a couple other spots just to be sure.

Type of Food	Target Temp
Poultry	165°
Salmon	125° -135°
Ground meat	165°
Steak	
Rare	120° to 130°
Medium rare	130° to 140°
Medium	140° to 150°
Ick	150° and up

Use fresh ingredients whenever you can. Lemon juice from a bottle will never be as good as the real thing, chicken broth from bouillon will never be as yummy, dried basil will taste, well, dry, and don't even get me started on garlic! Home cooking, even with those substitutions, though, will still be better than eating from a box, so don't stress about it, just do your best.

I have cookbooks, lots of them! I don't use them much, except for baking and then my favorites are really old ones from that I inherited from my Grandpa (yup, he was a great cook!). I do really like my Alton Brown Good Eats cookbooks for reference because they are more about teaching technique rather than just a list of recipes.

You can substitute seasoning salt for any recipe that calls for salt and pepper (S&P). My favorites are Jane's Krazy Mixed-Up Salt and Tony Chachere's Creole Seasoning (this is the one they have on the tables at The Back Porch restaurant in Destin, FL, one of my favorite restaurants anywhere).

A well-stocked spice rack makes life so much easier! The thing is though, it can be overwhelming when you go to the grocery store and see half an aisle of little jars, so I thought I would give my list of things I actually use on a regular basis. It is always best to buy the herbs and spices whole and grind, crush, chop, or grate them when you need them, especially if you plan to store them more than six months or so. I like the spice blends that come in a grinder because they are yummy and usually don't have weird ingredients to prevent caking and color loss and stuff. Some things are a pain to use or store whole, so I skip those but other things are so much better, like nutmeg, that it is worth the extra three square inches of storage space and 30 seconds of prep time to use whole.

Savory	Sweet
Garlic	Cinnamon
Jane's Krazy Salt	Cloves
Tony's Chachere's Creole Seasoning	Nutmeg (whole with grater)
Sea salt (in grinder)	Ginger
Peppercorns (in grinder)	Apple pie spice
Italian herb blend	Vanilla
Chili powder	Cocoa
Oregano	
Parsley	
Basil	
Rosemary	
Dill	
Curry powder	
Lemon pepper blend	
Steak pepper blend	
Salsa mix	
Crushed red pepper flakes	
Chicken bouillon	
Beef bouillon	

Why Do It? You might be thinking, "well, this seems like a lot and we haven't even gotten into the meat of it," but trust me - it is worth whatever uncomfortable moments there might be during your transition. Here are my top three reasons:

*Quality. Period.
*Easy. If you are lazy, like me, cooking at home with some simple prep work is easier than finding your shoes and keys and dragging a toddler anywhere, that's for sure!
*Self esteem - Being the one to feed your family from your own hands is amazing. Teaching your children how to care for themselves and the people they love gives a purpose to your life in a way that few other things do.

There are other great reasons to cook at home, too. It is really annoying for everyone involved to have an allergy when you eat out, making meals at home cuts out that risk and frustration. Plus, if you are eating at home, you control the ingredients making things almost always healthier. I'm not a fanatic, really. I know a lot of people who would be horrified by some of the things I'm fine with - yes, I know shortening is bad, it is also cheap and dairy free, so I'm using it - yes, I know that some people think cans cause cancer, I'm slowly starting to use more dried beans and freezing some tomatoes, but cans are just too easy, so I'm not giving them up - yes, I know making condiments is a thing, but I'm just fine with my store bought mayo, mustard, and barbecue sauce, and I'm for sure not giving up my Sriracha!

Chapter 3:

Meal Planning: How to Eat Like it's on Purpose

Meal planning is a big scary word, like budget, and test. I get it. But, done my way, I promise, it makes life so much easier and takes very little time to implement. Plus, it is my number one tip on how to save money on groceries.

It has been brought to my attention many times that it is unusual for a family to spend as little as I do (around $200/month) on groceries and still have delicious and even sometimes high-end meals.

Food for thought: The USDA calculates different costs for a healthy diet at home. The numbers from January 2014 for a family of four (two adults, two kids ages 7 and 10) range from a thrifty food plan of $148 a week to a liberal plan of $293 a week. I literally can not fathom spending that much per week, those seem like monthly numbers to me! The average food stamp allowance for a family of four is $133 per week, which even seems lavish. Please don't take that to mean that I support cutting benefits! It means to me that education is vitally necessary to ensure families can make it all month on whatever amount they have.

Let me say here, I talk a lot about how inexpensively we eat. What I am not always clear about is the motivation. Anyone who knows my husband or I will not be surprised by this: we have little to no self control. Asking us to deprive ourselves, especially for something as frivolous as staying within a budget would NEVER fly! So, let's start with our motivation:

The secret - we eat and plan and shop the way we do because of two incredibly selfish reasons -

Laziness and Snobbiness

*If you plan the month's meals in advance and shop so every ingredient is in the house, you can make dinner without having to put real pants and shoes on.
*I only have to think about what to have for dinner once a month!
*We are snobby eaters.
*We like the stuff we eat and think most processed food is gross.
*We want to have control over the kids' diets.

The awesome thing is that when I started keeping track of what I spent after beginning meal planning, I was pleasantly surprised to find out just how cheap it was! It is rare that you find such a nice perk to being lazy and snobby!

There are many ways to meal plan ranging from very unstructured to militarily precise. Obviously, I go with the bare minimum effort that still gets results. I prefer a monthly list and keep it on a whiteboard in the kitchen. I only plan one meal per day (actually less since some recipes make 8-12 servings so we use them for several days), but make enough for lunch leftovers and also always have ingredients for snacks and simple lunches on hand. Once you make your list of everything you will eat for the month, it's just a matter of grocery shopping so that all ingredients are available for all meals on list. That way the kids or I can pick from the list each day and then just erase the choice. Pretty low-tech, but it works for us. Near the end of the month there are fewer options, but we rarely have issues with being unable to find something we like.

Just because you are eating at home doesn't mean you can't make the things you love from the packages and restaurants. You can not make McDonald's fries at home. Other than that, just about everything else can be made at home for cheaper, with fewer questionable ingredients, and usually in very little time. Think about it, when you order food at a restaurant, the kitchen makes it (along with dozens of other people's food at the same time) usually in under 15 minutes. Remember, the secret is having the ingredients prepped, but you can totally do it!

It might seem unlikely (or even overwhelming), but by following simple meal planning strategies and also learning easy ways to convert fast food/restaurant/pre-packaged meals into healthier, faster, and cheaper homemade versions is easy.

Some examples of meals and why I chose them from our typical meals:

Reasons to Cook at Home	Examples
Make-at-home fast food or restaurant food (and where I stole the dish)	Salmon nuggets with spicy aioli (a little Cajun restaurant that closed) Chicken alfredo (every chain or Italian restaurant ever) Jambalaya (our trips to Destin, FL) Curry (every Indian restaurant)
Allergies (I am dairy free, but all allergies are safer at home)	Pizza Desserts
Healthier choices (I substitute whole wheat flour and no preservatives obviously)	Pot pie Biscuits Desserts
Taste preference	Everything! Make it how you like it!

While you make your list, think about ingredient pairing, particularly produce. What's that? Well, make sure you are using all of your ingredients to their best potential. For instance, I buy fresh produce and try to use it before it starts to wilt, but as soon as it starts to go south, I dice, portion, and freeze it, or use it for stock, or (for tomatoes and red peppers) slow roast, pack in olive oil, and freeze. But ideally, I will have planned so that I make things that use similar ingredients, but are totally different dishes on subsequent days. Think outside the box here!

Examples:
*I make a cold pasta salad with onion, tomato, and cucumber. I also need half a cucumber for sushi, so I try to make those within a couple of days of each other.
*I try to remember to make stock (which uses bones, onion, celery, and carrot) on the same day that I make onion heavy pasta or soup so I can use the ends of the onion in the stock. If I'm really lucky, stock day will fall on the day that I also have some floppy carrots and celery ready to be used.
*Cold black bean salsa and fajitas use many of the same ingredients.
*Tomato paste. Even those tiny cans seem like too much most of the time, but if I use a spoonful one day, then I either throw the rest in a jar in the freezer or make a pot of marinara to use for pizza, spaghetti, or to dip garlic bread.
*Deviled eggs pair with tuna salad (or any salad).
*Granola makes fruit and yogurt into parfaits.
*We make a lot of muffins, usually pumpkin. One recipe uses about half a can, so I usually double the recipe and freeze the extras, but sometimes I will use the pumpkin to thicken a vegetable soup or pasta.

I recommend choosing some meals that you love in restaurants and then breaking them down to figure out how to make them at home, adding in some new recipes, and then filling out the month with old favorites. The following is a full month's meals and snacks. If you had absolutely no food in the house (no seasonings, no mayo, etc.) then you would need to buy a few more things, but for the most part, this list will completely feed a family of four for a month.

Trust me, I know it doesn't seem that way, but it really will (the snacks are the key)! In the Grocery Shopping chapter, on page 19, the entire shopping list, with prices is shown and detailed recipes are in the Recipes chapter.

My typical meals:

Main dishes - in no particular order and without sides listed

Name of Dish	Number of Meals Recipe Makes	Times I will Make in the Month
Meatball subs	1	1
Lentil loaf	2	1
Spaghetti	2	1
Steak and potatoes	1	1
Chicken and dumplings	2	1
Chicken pot pie (9x13 pan)	2	2
Chili	2	1
Tomato and bean pasta	2	1
Chicken alfredo	2	1
Potato salsa chicken	1	2
Frittata	1	1
Salmon nuggets	1	1
Salmon	1	1
Fried shrimp	1	1
Vegetable bean pasta	2	1
Chicken and veg pasta	2	1
Chicken curry	2	1
White bean chicken chili	2	1
Jambalaya	2	1

My snack list (some homemade, some store bought)

Name of Snack	HM or SB or Both	Number of Recipes Made or Packages Purchased
Hummus	Both	1 SB or 2 HM
Tuna Salad	HM	2
Chips – pita, tortilla	Both	3
Pretzels	SB	1
Granola	HM	3
Peanut butter	SB	1
Trail mix	HM	2
Cereal	SB	2
Bean dip	HM	2
Cookies	HM	2
Bread/biscuits	Both	3
Fruit	Fresh & dried	a lot
Oatmeal Packets	HM	2
Pumpkin muffins	HM	2
Yogurt	SB	1
Frozen vegetables	SB	1
Frozen fruit	SB	1
Crackers	Both	6

I should expand on some of these items, I suppose, so in no particular order:

*I have babysat for a lot of toddlers and also have my own. They all love eating frozen peas and mixed vegetables (just microwaved for 15 seconds so they aren't hard as rocks) for snacks. I am certain that it is not a fluke that I have the only kids who would eat this, give it a shot!

*I have a weakness for the Aldi hummus four-pack, it is better than any other brand I have tried (and I've tried a lot!) and honestly, better than my homemade. It is certainly more expensive than making my own, so I go back and forth on this convenience item.

*We eat lots of crackers, my 18 year old has a bit of an addiction, I'm afraid. I make them from scratch sometimes and they are delicious and cheap, but take forever, so it is more of a fun activity (I get to use the pasta roller!) rather than a practical substitute.

*We only eat cereal dry and as snacks, it isn't nutritious or filling enough to eat for breakfast.

*We make oatmeal packets to eat almost every day, 1/2C oats, 1-2t brown sugar, hearty shake of cinnamon, dash of salt all in a little baggie. In the morning we just add 1C of water and microwave for 3 minutes, ta da, a healthy and delicious breakfast for next to nothing!

*I buy a large container of plain yogurt. Lucille eats it as a snack with a small spoonful of jelly to sweeten. Paige adds it to smoothies. It also works as a sour cream substitute.

*We always have cookies either made and in the freezer; or mixed and frozen in logs to quick bake; or as a premade mix with everything in a baggie except the egg; or just have the ingredients ready. My sweet tooth is a doozy, but I have found some tricks to tame it. I often grab a cookie when I pass where they are, so I try to keep them out of sight. Also, I make really small cookies, I used to make one to two tablespoon sized cookies, but I found that if I make them with one teaspoon of dough, they come out about silver dollar size and are just perfect to soothe my craving.

*We make muffins, biscuits, tortillas, and bread a lot to munch on, so those ingredients are included in the grocery list.

*We put peanut butter on everything from crackers to bread to celery to spoons (to Peeps, but only for mom) to...

Every family's list will be different, but if you are on the fence about changing your ways, just use my menu, grocery list, and recipes as a thirty day challenge. After the first month, I know it will be easier to make your own menus.

This is what we would eat in a typical month if we all ate at home the entire month. I comfortably claim that this amount of food will feed a family of two adults and two any age kids. In practice, we don't all five eat here all three meals every day.

Factors in our budget:

*We are making an effort to eat healthier and that means, among other things, less meat. If you are unwilling to even try the recipes as listed (but, really, what do you have to lose, just try it already!), you just go right ahead and double the meat, it will still be healthier, cheaper, and taste better when you make it at home. If you would like to use less meat, a secret is to cut it into very tiny pieces and serve in pasta, potato, or rice dishes; that way you get a little bit with each bite.
*We usually go out to eat three or four times, that usually (but not always) comes from the household budget, not the grocery budget.
*Sometimes the neighbor girls come over to eat, so we feed 1-3 extra a few meals a month.
*Usually one teen eats breakfast at his dad's and both eat dinner there a couple times a week.
*We feed a toddler and even though toddlers don't eat an adult-size serving, they waste a lot and throw almost as much as they eat on the floor!
*Our lightest eater is actually the husband, he works in a restaurant and often eats one or even two meals a day at work.
*The kicker, though, and why I am confident almost any family can feel full is - me. I am a relatively small person, but I EAT. Like, an impressive and embarrassing amount and I am here all day every day.

Chapter 4:

Emergency Meal Planning

But, what if you are hit with an unexpected expense and have to REALLY cut back? This is what I would do. Notice that I don't cut out all the meat, or all the snacks, even cookies! Just because things aren't going your way doesn't mean you should have to do without all the good stuff. As a matter of fact, if things aren't going well, you might need more cookies! There is no reason to feel deprived the whole month (or months), you can still eat delicious food, the only difference is that it might not be as varied as when you have more money. That being said, remember, changing up the spices can make two dishes with the same ingredients seem way different! Whole chicken is by far the most economical meat, especially considering the stock you can easily make that will make the bean dishes feel more "meaty". Ideally, you have been slowly building up your pantry and freezer so that you could absorb a grocery budget cut without much changing at least for a month or so. My emergency list assumes you have some condiments and spices. But, it also includes some food not used in the recipes to fill in if you want to change things or add more meat. It goes a tad over $100 because when we did a real-life simulation we needed to add a couple of things, but you could scale back some if absolutely necessary. See the shopping list on page 21. For a more in depth look at our Thrifty Month, check my blog at myfamilybz.blogspot.com.

Could you spend less? Yes, but if you are in a situation where you have less than $100 to use for groceries for your family for more than a month or two, then you could, and should seek assistance, that's what it is for.

What if you only have $100?

Thrifty Meals

Name of Dish	Number of Meals Recipe Makes	Times I will Make in the Month
Lentil loaf	2	1
Spaghetti	2	1
Chicken and dumplings	2	1
Chicken pot pie (9x13 pan)	2	2
Chili	2	1
Tomato and bean pasta	2	1
Chicken alfredo pasta	2	1
Potato salsa chicken	1	2
Frittata	1	1
Diced potato with chk alfredo	2	1
Baked potato with chili	1	1
Scrambled eggs and pancakes	1	1
Vegetable bean pasta	2	1
Chicken and veg pasta	2	1
White bean curry	2	1
White bean chicken chili	2	1
Beans and Rice	2	1

Thrifty snack list

Name of Snack	HM or SB or Both	Number of Recipes Made or Packages Purchased
Tuna Salad	HM	1
Chips – tortilla	Both	1
Pretzels	SB	1
Granola	HM	2
Peanut butter	SB	1
Peanuts	SB	2
Bean dip	HM	2
Cookies	HM	2
Bread	Both	3
Bananas	SB	20
Oatmeal Packets	HM	30
Pumpkin muffins	HM	2
Raisins	SB	1
Frozen vegetables	SB	1
Saltines	Both	3
Apples	SB	12

Chapter 5:

Grocery Shopping: More Fun than Shoe Shopping (if you're me)

Let's start this chapter with a rant, shall we. This is the money chapter, the nerd in me LOVES this time - I get to prove my stuff! And I want to scream when people tell me McDonalds and Little Caesars are cheaper than cooking at home. It certainly isn't (see the chart below). Look!

Cost Comparisons

Sample Items from our Basic Shopping List	Cost per serving
Carrots $.35/lb (4 servings)	.09
Canned beans $.70/can (3.5 servings)	.20
Eggs $1.50/dz	.13
Tilapia or cod $3/lb	.75
Salmon $4/lb	1.00
Chicken, whole $1.25/lb	.31
Pasta, dried $1/lb (8 servings)	.13
Potatoes $.35/lb (2 servings)	.17
Rice, brown $1/lb (11 servings)	.09
Frozen veggies $1.00/lb (6 servings)	.17
Canned tomatoes $.70/can (3.5 servings)	.20
Whole wheat bread - $3/16 slices	.19
Oatmeal $2.29/30 servings	.08
Dried fruit $2/8 servings	.25
Vanilla yogurt $3.30/2 lb (6 servings)	.55
Apples $1/lb (about 3 apples)	.33

Meal Options You Can Make With the Items or Buy at McD or LC (with cost per serving)
Homemade:
Salmon, rice, veggies, apples - $1.59
Egg, oatmeal with dried fruit, toast - $.65
Tomato and bean pasta, carrots - $.62
Chicken noodle soup w/veg, yogurt – $1.16
McDonald's:
McDouble, fries $2.50
Little Caesar's:
Single topping pizza $1.59 (3.5 servings per pizza)

So, let's get to it - what are the grocery shopping rules?

*Only (mostly) buy ingredients - buy as few pre-packaged things as you can, before you put something in your cart, try to imagine if it is worth it to make it from scratch.

*Remember to take your list with you!

*Be open to change if there is a good sale or something sounds good.

*Use any extra money to stock pantry.

*What about coupons? I keep meaning to do that...but...two things:
--They are mostly for processed foods
--I'm lazy

*Have a list of all the things you ever buy at the store to help make your list (I call this my Master List).

Master List Discussion:

I love to grocery shop. I know, that's weird, but I do. I really, really do. I get excited about lists and comparison shopping and meal planning. I couldn't care less about shoe or clothes shopping; I'm not a good girl... Anyway, I have some tools that I use that make it more fun for me, but also could make it faster and easier for someone less passionate about groceries (I hear that's a thing).

My favorite is the Master List. I made a list of everything I ever buy (and put it on the fridge) so when I make my shopping list I don't forget anything. This is only practical because of one thing - I only buy ingredients. When I bought pre-made sauces and boxed meals my list was twice as long, but could only produce half as many meals. I do rely a lot on cans, specifically canned tomatoes, but they are so versatile! Salsa? Marinara? Tomato basil pasta? Roasted tomato crostinis? Jambalaya? All from one can? Come on! That's awesome!

Every once in a while we will make a recipe that calls for something else (sushi comes to mind) and some things on the list are rare purchases, and, of course, most of the dairy items listed are actually dairy free versions. I recognize other people probably have other staples that they can't believe I live without, but we are doing a-okay. :-)

Without further ado, the list:

PRODUCE	CANS	CONDIMENTS	BAKING
fuji apples	diced toms	mayonnaise	flour
green apples	crushed toms	mustard	shortening
oranges/clem	tom sauce	ketchup	oil
grapes	rotel	barbecue	olive oil
strawberries	pineapple	salsa	Pam
dried fruit	mand. oranges	soy sauce	yeast
avocado	mushrooms	Worcestershire	sugar
tomatoes	pumpkin	peanut butter	brown sugar
r/o/y/g peppers	black beans	jelly	powdered sugar
celery	white beans	vinegar	salt
carrots	chick peas	apple cider vin	coarse salt
lettuce	chili beans	balsamic vin	pepper
spinach/greens	kidney beans	relish	spices
potatoes	pinto beans		baking soda
sweet potatoes	refried beans		baking powder
onions	yams		vanilla
mushrooms	tuna		honey
asparagus			pudding
lemons			jiffy cornbread
limes			
herbs			
garlic			
DAIRY	PASTA, etc	FROZEN	MEAT
butter	rotini	broccoli	salmon
sour cream	shells	Cali veg	tuna
cream cheese	penne	pot pie veg	chicken
yogurt	spaghetti	edamame	shrimp
soymilk	quinoa	asian veg	steak
eggs	brown rice	hash potatoes	deli
tofu	cous cous	corn	pepperoni
orange juice	egg noodle	green beans	
	lentils	peas	
	dried beans	fruit	
		cool whip	
CEREAL	BREAD	PAPER	OTHER
cheerios	sliced	toilet paper	coffee
shredded wheat	crackers	saran wrap	juice
oats	tortillas	foil	nuts
	loaf	parchment	
	buns	snack Ziploc	
		sandwich Ziploc	
		bowl covers	

Grocery list with approximate prices for typical month (listed in Meal Planning chapter):

2.00	flour (5 lb)
1.50	baking powder
0.10	salt
2.90	shortening
3.00	milk
3.00	eggs (2 dz)
4.60	old fash oats (2)
1.00	sour cream
2.60	olive oil
2.00	vegetable oil
1.70	bouillon cubes
1.80	yogurt
1.50	brown sugar
1.60	sugar
2.50	honey
2.00	seasonings
4.75	steak (12 oz)
3.50	ground beef (1 lb)
8.00	salmon (8 filets)
5.00	med. shrimp (1 lb)
3.00	andouille sausage
8.00	whole chicken (2/4-5 lb)
6.00	chick thighs(6 thighs)
1.50	French bread
2.20	hoagies
1.50	sandwich bread
2.00	frozen mix veg (32 oz)
5.00	frozen CA blend veg (60 oz)
4.00	frozen juice (2)
2.50	frozen strawberries
1.00	frozen corn (16 oz)
1.00	frozen peas (16 oz)
5.00	pasta (5 lb)
1.00	spaghetti (1 lb)
1.00	rice (2 lb)
1.00	lentils (1 lb)
1.90	pretzels
4.00	cashews
4.00	peanuts
1.90	peanut butter
4.00	hummus
3.50	raisins
1.50	mixed dried berries
1.20	tortilla chips
2.00	pita chips
10.00	coffee

2.00		shredded wheat
2.00		straw preserves
1.70		jar alfredo sauce
7.00		crackers (5 boxes)
1.20		carrots (2 lb)
1.40		celery (1 stalk)
2.00		onions (3 lb)
2.30		potatoes (5 lb)
2.60		mini bell peppers
0.50		green bell pepper
8.00		apples (20)
5.00		mandarin oranges (1 box)
2.50		bananas (20)
0.90		cilantro
2.00		spring greens
1.00		garlic
2.40		can beans (4)
1.80		can chili beans (3)
0.90		can pumpkin
1.40		can tuna (2)
0.80		refried beans
0.50		can black olives
0.50		tomato paste
2.40		can diced tomatoes (56 oz)
2.00		can crushed tomatoes (56 oz)
1.00		tomato sauce (32 oz)
190.55		TOTAL

Grocery List Notes:
*The bulk of my prices are from Aldi or are store brand items.
*I buy organic produce when it is reasonable, but most of the prices here are conventionally grown products.
*We probably actually spend another $10ish on fruit a month, but most families would be fine with the amount listed.
*The teen boy is seriously addicted to crackers, so we buy more than most people, I also make some and he still wishes we had more.
*We are drinkers here :-) but booze has its own budget, so I don't include it.

Grocery list with approximate prices for thrifty month (listed in Emergency Meal Planning chapter):

4.00	flour (10 lb)
1.00	baking powder
0.10	salt
2.90	shortening
3.00	milk (1 gal)
4.50	eggs (3 dz)
4.60	old fash oats (2)
1.20	brown sugar
2.60	olive oil
2.00	vegetable oil
1.70	bouillon cubes
1.60	sugar
1.00	tomato sauce (32 oz)
0.40	tomato paste
2.40	can diced tomatoes (4/14 oz)
2.00	can crushed tomatoes (2/28 oz)
1.20	carrots (2 lb)
1.40	celery (1 stalk)
2.00	onions (3 lb)
2.30	potatoes (5 lb)
2.50	bananas (20)
3.00	apples (12)
.90	green bell pepper (4)
1.00	garlic
2.00	sandwich bread (2)
1.80	can chili beans (3)
0.90	can pumpkin
1.40	can tuna (2)
0.80	refried beans
2.00	frozen mix veg (32 oz)
5.00	CA blend veg (60 oz)
1.00	frozen corn (16 oz)
1.00	frozen peas (16 oz)
12.00	whole chicken (3/4-5 lb)
1.50	rice (3 lb)
1.00	lentils (1 lb)
1.80	penne pasta (2 lb)
1.50	elbow pasta (2 lb)
1.00	spaghetti (1 lb)
7.50	dried beans (6 lb)
2.00	peanuts
1.70	peanut butter
1.20	tortilla chips
1.25	raisins
1.70	jar alfredo sauce
2.70	crackers (3 boxes)
102.05	TOTAL

Chapter 6:

Prepping and Freezer Meals

I'm going to go against the fray a bit here. Right now, the blogosphere, magazines, and TV seem to be obsessed with once a month cooking (OAMC) and freezer meals. I am less impressed. Making full meals for the freezer often requires remembering to take it out a day ahead to thaw or baking for an hour or more, both of which aren't appealing to me. They also take up more space in the freezer, require more expensive storage containers, and the most popular recipes are frequently made with less healthy ingredients than I like to use. Am I going to yell at you for making some freezer meals? Of course not, but I just don't think they are as magnificent as I keep reading they are.

What *would* I recommend? Prepping! Notice what items you use most often and in what form they are. You will likely notice a lot of overlap. I have put together my lists below - where they are stored is in parentheses (F)reezer, (R)efrigerator, (P)antry:

ESSENTIAL	DARN HANDY	NICE TO HAVE
chicken, cooked and diced (F)	marinara or spaghetti sauce (F)	cookie dough (F)
chicken stock (F)	chili (F)	vegetable base (F)
onion, diced (R)	alfredo sauce (F)	pasta (F)
peppers, diced (F)	andouille sausage, sliced and browned (F)	biscuit mix (F or R)
carrots, diced (F)	ground beef, browned (F)	pesto (F)
celery, diced (F)	trail mix (P)	roasted tomatoes (F)
dried beans (F)	ham, small diced (F)	roasted peppers (F)
granola (P)	cookies (F)	bread, cubes, slices, and loaves (F)
chocolate truffles (F) (yeah, vital. it's my list)	bread crumbs (F)	hummus (F)

Notes;
*I usually put the carrots and celery in the same zip top bag because every recipe I have that calls for one, calls for both.
*I like to have the red sauce portioned in two sizes, one for putting over pasta, and a smaller one for dipping bread, mini pizzas, and topping meatball subs.
*I soak the beans, then cook them about an hour before freezing; that way, they only take about another half hour to finish cooking.
*Alfredo sauce, I buy one jar, divide it into three containers, then when I use it for pasta, I use olive oil, chicken broth, and seasonings, then add the alfredo at the very end. This stretches the sauce, reduces the amount of dairy, and lets me adjust the flavor to our family's garlic loving preference.
*I rarely pre-cook my pasta, but every once in a while I will throw a handful into a soup to cool it down or use it for a quick toddler snack.
*Keep your onions in a mason jar or the whole refrigerator will be onion flavored.
*I make vegetable base by pureeing vegetable soup (even when the soup isn't the best, it still makes a good starter) then freeze it flat in a zip top bag. To use, I just break off a chunk.
*Any time I have bread about to be stale, I crumble it up and add it to a bag in the freezer, then I use the crumbs to make meatballs, lentil loaf, and to top casseroles.

Is my freezer as fancy and beautiful as those OAMC freezers? Nope, not even close, here it is on a good day:

Photo by Stephanie Scott-Huffman

When:
I usually do about two big shopping trips a month on Saturdays and then do my prepping on Sundays. I spend several hours on prep, but a lot of it isn't terribly hands on (like cooking the chicken, beans, chili, or sauce). When I used to shop more often it was harder to prep all at once so I would do smaller prep tasks whenever I could fit them in. I also save a lot of time by making double batches of dinner throughout the week. We use dinner leftovers for lunch the next day.

Why:
I can't stress enough the importance of having a stocked pantry and freezer! I rarely, rarely, rarely spend more than 15 minutes getting dinner on the table because I don't have to do all the chopping every night. If there is anything I need to chop, I make sure I chop extra to put in the freezer or fridge for later.

How:
Most things in my lists are pretty self-explanatory usually, just dice into the size that your family likes, drop in a zip top bag, label and throw in the freezer. If you aren't familiar with cooking a whole chicken, I get that it might seem complicated. It isn't, I promise! This is where the bulk of our protein comes from every week. It sounds mundane, but we don't feel like it's the same all the time - and we like chicken.

Whole Chicken

This is the most detailed way to cook a chicken, but feel free to skip any steps you don't feel like doing and it will still taste good.

• • •

Pull out any giblets or neck from the chicken and save for later. You can bake the chicken plain or with some seasonings sprinkled on and in the chicken.

I like to add some herbs and spices under the skin, this is a bit messy, but makes it super yummy – remember, you are completely washable! Put about two tablespoons of olive oil in a bowl, add herbs (chopped fresh if you have them) and/or spices and garlic. Almost anything will work, really. I always use garlic and of course ground salt and pepper, and then add other things like basil, or lemon-pepper seasoning or rosemary or other seasoning blends. Use whatever you have. Use your hands to pull the skin away from the chicken and slide the oil/herb mix under the skin all over the chicken. Also, add some to the inside cavity.

Photo by Stephanie Scott-Huffman

For the actual baking, I usually use my pressure cooker, but the oven works fine, it is just easier to overcook it. Make sure you are using your probe thermometer! Put the chicken in a 9x13 or so pan with about two cups of chicken broth that you made yourself and saved (see below), two cubes of bouillon dissolved in the water, or canned or boxed broth. Cover the whole pan with foil and put in a 350º oven for about 1-1 1/2 hours (for a 3-4 pound bird). Cook covered until the thermometer reads 160º then take the foil off and turn the oven up to 450º. The temperature should reach 165º right about the time the skin turns nice and brown. Remove from the oven and let rest for at least 15 minutes. If you skip this step it will be dry.

Use the chicken in any of the ways in the Recipe chapter or just slice it and eat it plain. Even if you are eating it like that, there will still be plenty to make at least one more meal out of, so pull any scraps of meat off the bone and save for later. I usually get about one sandwich size zip top bag of meat per pound of chicken. I consider this a meal size portion for any of my recipes written to make 6-8 servings.

When you have pulled most of the meat off the bones, put the carcass in a pot with any juices left over from cooking and the giblets and neck from earlier and add water until it is completely covered. Add some celery stalks, onion and carrots if you have some handy (they don't even need to be chopped). Add a splash of vinegar (I use apple cider vinegar) to help pull calcium from the bones and into the stock. Cover and simmer for an hour or more, stirring occasionally. Even easier, put all of this in the crock pot on low overnight.

Strain out the carcass and stuff and discard (after checking for any small pieces of meat). After it completely cools, it will look like chicken flavored Jell-o, lovely visual, huh? If you are concerned about fat, then you can put the stock in the refrigerator or freezer and the fat will harden on top and you can just lift it off. I will say though, that I leave it with all the fat and here is why: fat is delicious. That should be enough, but if you need more, I have more: we choose to eat very small portions of meat because it is a healthier way to eat, even making many meals with beans or tofu as the protein; because of that, we have more room in our diet for things like fats and oils. Fat is also filling and making otherwise meatless dishes with stock makes them feel "meatier" which satisfies the staunch meat eaters in the family.

Golden delicious stock!

Stretching Chicken is what I do most days. I am a huge proponent of whole chicken, but the same techniques can be used with inexpensive thighs or leg quarters, which are juicy and delicious!

First, why should you stretch the chicken?

Let's start here: Average Americans eat WAY too much meat, in my opinion, and I am in pretty good company in that opinion. Nearly every organization that deals with health and nutrition agrees that a serving of meat should be between two and four ounces and some groups think even less!

So how does my family meet those recommendations most days? Taking what appear to be single serving size pieces and turning them into family servings:

Look, two thighs= two servings, right?   Yum, two delicious servings...

But wait! When you take the meat off the bone, it magically turns into enough for a family!

Bonus, you get bones and skin to make a small pot of crock pot stock!

Look! 2 cups of rice, 16 ounces of frozen vegetables, and about 1 1/2 pounds of cooked chicken (about 2 cups). Six to eight very hearty servings! So, go forth and stretch your chicken!

Chapter 7:

Recipes and Techniques

There is a common theme in all of my techniques – try to dirty as few dishes as possible.

Pasta, pasta, pasta, I LOVE it! It is versatile, easy, delicious, only uses one pan, perfect!

I always try to use as little water as possible to boil my pasta in so that I can season it while the pasta is cooking instead of waiting until it is done. This does three things, it reduces the possibility of ending up with mushy pasta, it saves time, and it makes the pasta taste better. Use just enough water to cover the amount of pasta you will be using and as it cooks, it should absorb most of the water and any flavors you've added. You will have to stir it more often if using this method to keep it from sticking to the bottom and keep it all covered in the liquid. Most pasta takes 12 minutes to cook so at about the 8 minute mark, I add frozen vegetables (they retain more nutrients than fresh unless you get them freshly picked, plus are quicker and don't spoil, like I tend to let fresh do) and fully cooked meat (if starting from raw, then you would add it at the very beginning and let it cook with the pasta). When the water comes back to a boil, the pasta should be done and the vegetables should be cooked through. Then all you need to do is add about a tablespoon of cornstarch dissolved in two-ish ounces of cold water, broth, or wine right at the end, bring it to a quick simmer and voila! a finished dish. Even better than starting with water, is broth. Either the homemade chicken broth from your whole baked chicken experience or store bought, or at least add some bouillon. Ninety percent of the pasta I make is chicken based, but beef broth also makes tasty pasta.

Remember that the pasta is going to keep cooking after you serve it so make sure it is still a little firm (al dente is the fancy name).

Fried Things

Fried foods are yummy. They're not healthy and nothing you do to them makes them that way, but sometimes, you just need some fat, ya know? Honestly, I usually just give up on making a real meal and have fried food day be a snack-as-you-cook meal. You can put the pieces that are finished in the oven set to about 250º to keep them warm, but they will never be as good as eating them as soon as they're not lava-fire hot. Today, we ate them with some grapes and raw veggies as I cooked.

The target food isn't really important; it's all about the technique. This is a messy ordeal, so make sure there are some helpers around to clean up. You will need three bowls, a cookie sheet, a cooling rack, and some paper towels or pages from an old phonebook. If you have a deep fryer, then it will be set to 350º, otherwise use a heavy pan and a thermometer set to 350º. I like to use half shortening and half vegetable oil. But, I'm getting ahead of myself. Prepping the food before you turn the oil on will make a better product.

I use a three step breading:
-First bowl is plain flour
-Second is an egg and about a cup of milk (I, of course, use soy) whisked together
-Third bowl is flour mixed with a lot of Cajun seasoning (you could also use breadcrumbs or crushed cornflakes)

With each bowl dredge the food through and shake it off. Then - and this is a super important, often skipped step - put the food on a cookie sheet or cooling rack and let it set for at least ten minutes, longer is even better. This waiting period does some magic thing that makes the breading not fall off or be mushy.

What to fry? Onion rings, shrimp, scallops, calamari (chicken tenders, broccoli, green beans, okra, almost anything!)
I like to slice vidalia onions into really skinny rings for frying

No more than a handful of things in the oil at once!   Calamari and skinny onion rings take about 1 minute, scallops about 2 minutes and shrimp about 3-4 minutes.

Potato Chips
These are so easy! Just use a potato peeler to make lots of super thin slices. Drop them in water until you're ready to fry and then use a salad spinner or towels to get them totally dry. Drop a very small handful into the oil and swish them around to separate and fry for about one minute. Pull them out with a metal slotted spoon and immediately sprinkle with plain or seasoned salt.

Appetizers, Breads, and Side Dishes

Mashed or Cubed Potatoes	
potatoes sour cream butter chicken bouillon or broth chopped fresh herbs (parsley, cilantro, chives, rosemary, etc.), optional s&p	Cut the potatoes into about 1 inch cubes and boil with a little salt and a drizzle of oil (to help keep it from boiling over). When they smoosh easily with a fork, drain them and add the ingredients and either mash or just stir and leave most of the cubes intact. You can try adding a little lime zest (use a grater to get just the dark green off the lime) and a squeeze of lime juice for a different twist. I like it this way, hubby doesn't, but I think you should give it a try sometime.

Black Bean Salsa	
black beans, canned or dried that have been cooked, drained and rinsed frozen corn red, yellow, orange, and green bell peppers (or any combination you have) handful of chopped cilantro olive oil juice of a lime s&p	Chop the peppers into small pieces (most kids love dicing, get them involved!). You can add as many or as few peppers and corn as you want, I usually have roughly half beans and half other things. This is best served with the scoop style tortilla chips. If you make this within a couple of days of making the stir fry I describe later you can slice the remaining peppers into strips and add them to that or put them on a veggie tray with some ranch and carrots and broccoli or such – food pairing.

Hummus	
1 (15-ounce) can chickpeas, also known as garbanzo beans, drained and rinsed 2 medium garlic cloves Juice of 1 medium lemon 1/4 c roasted tahini (I rarely actually have tahini, so I skip it or drizzle about 1/2 t of sesame oil) 1/4 c olive oil water if it needs it to blend well S&P	Throw everything but the olive oil into the food processor and start it up, drizzle in the olive oil and water (if needed) and process until smooth. Sometimes I add one or more of the following: a teaspoon or so of cayenne or smoked paprika 1/4 c diced onion or green onion 1/2 c fresh parsley 5-6 oven roasted tomatoes

Bean Dip	
salsa can refried beans	We buy a salsa mix from the farmer's market that just mixes with diced or crushed tomatoes, but any salsa will do. Add about half as much as the amount of beans and warm it up. It's so easy and the kids will eat it as a meal every day if I let them.

Steamed Vegetables	
any frozen vegetable seasoned salt optional: olive oil or butter	Put in a bowl, cover with plastic wrap, 2 minutes in a microwave – ta da!

Garlic Bread	
loaf bread, sliced olive oil or butter garlic, minced s&p or Krazy Jane's	Put olive oil or butter in a bowl with the garlic and seasoning, microwave it for about 45 seconds, brush or drizzle it over any bread and bake wrapped in foil or lay slices on pan and broil.

Asparagus	
fresh asparagus olive oil s&p	Cut or break about an inch off the bottom of all the stalks. I like to break it- it snaps right where the woody, tough part is. Hubby likes to use a knife because it's faster. Roll it in a little olive oil and dust with s&p and just put it under the broiler or in a medium-high skillet for 5 ish minutes, moving it around so it doesn't burn. Don't over cook it! It should be bright green with just a few grill marks and still pretty firm, not too droopy.

Biscuits	
2 C flour 1 T baking powder ½ t salt ½ C shortening 1 C milk	Preheat oven to 400 °. Combine dry ingredients, cut in shortening (rub it between your fingers until the shortening is all mixed with the flour mixture). You can stop at this point and put the mix in a bag or container ready to use later or continue on. Add milk (it will be sticky), press out on floured surface into a roughly 8 inch square, cut into 12 pieces and bake 8-10 minutes or until biscuits are golden brown.

Tortillas	
2 ½ C flour 1 t salt 3 T shortening 1 ¼ C hot water	Combine flour and salt, cut in shortening (rub it between your fingers until the shortening is all mixed with the flour mixture). Add hot water, knead for 2 minutes. Divide into 8-12 balls. Roll out very flat. Cook in hot skillet (med-high) about one minute on each side.

Basic Yeast Bread

8 oz milk plus 8 oz water
4 t yeast
1/3 C sugar or 2 T honey

2 egg yolks
2 oz olive oil
2 t salt
4 C flour plus 2 C flour

Warm the water on the stove or in microwave to 110* (just barely warm to the touch

mix milk, water, sugar or honey and yeast and let sit 5ish minutes (until the top is foamy), then add the rest and stir.

It is hard to say how much flour exactly, you are looking for a slightly sticky dough, but the exact amount changes with the temperature and humidity of the room and the attitude of the ingredients and the alignment of the stars and... and... I add 4 cups then dump onto a cup of flour on the counter and start kneading, adding more flour as I go, usually 6ish cups total. The dough is done when it can be kneaded without sticking to your hands too badly and the skin of it breaks and pocks when you push on it. That is a really poor description and I'm pretty sure that you shouldn't use the same words in a recipe as you might to describe disease, but there ya go; I did.

Put the dough ball in an oiled bowl, cover with a towel and put on top of the refrigerator (that's what the old women do and they know stuff) or in an oven with a proof setting (what the young, hip women, like myself use). Let it rise until it basically doubles in size (45-75 minutes) then dump it onto a floured counter. Now your dough is ready to become about 15 dinner rolls, two loaves, or 20 cinnamon rolls.

Shape the dough for your desired application and let rise another 30-60 minutes. Why such a large time frame? Remember the stars and attitude and humidity and all that jazz? It messes with the rise just like it messes with how much flour the liquid will soak up.

It sounds complicated, I promise, it really is easier than it seems!

Fun things to do with dough:

For cinnamon rolls:
Gently roll out the dough into a large rectangle (roughly 16"x20") and slather it in softened butter or margarine. I mean, really slather, like twice as much as you think is enough. At least 1/2 cup, probably more, just don't tell your nutritionist. Then add about 1/2 pound (1/4 bag) of dark brown sugar (I'm sure brown sugar is healthy...) and a big time amount of cinnamon. We are cinnamon lovers here and use a lot, probably at least 2T, just sprinkle it all over. Go all the way to the edges! Then carefully roll up the dough, slice into about 1" slices and put in greased pans. I use a 9"x13" pan and put 15 in it and then put the rest in a loaf pan.

For hummus rolls:
I invented these and I love them. Paige hates them, Levi accepts them, Doug likes them.

Roll out the dough like for cinnamon rolls, but put this instead:

Seasoned salt, smoked paprika, and pepper over the dough, then layer hummus, spinach leaves, fresh cilantro, onions, avocado chunks, and roasted tomatoes. After you roll and slice, top them with chopped kalamata olives and Italian dressing.

Dressings

I don't think America will have really made it until we have our own salad dressing. Until then we're stuck behind the French, Italians, Russians and Caesarians.
~Pat McNelis

Ranch	Honey Mustard
1/2 C mayo 1/2 C sour cream (real or dairy-free) 1/2 tsp dried dill 1/2 tsp dried parsley 1 clove garlic, pressed 1 piece onion (the size of a medium garlic clove), pressed in garlic press 1/8 tsp salt 1/8 tsp pepper	honey mustard (seriously, you can't mess this up)

Thousand Island	Oil and Vinegar
1-2 T ketchup 1 C mayonnaise 1 T sweet pickle relish	Olive oil splash of red wine vinegar seasoning salt

Entrees

"What are the two things they tell you are healthiest to eat? Chicken and fish, ... You know what you should do? Combine them ... eat a penguin."
-Dave Attell

Sorry, Dave, no penguin.

Chicken

Remember that chicken that you baked whole and picked all the meat off of in Chapter 6? It is perfect to use in any of the recipes below. You can use as much or as little chicken as you have. You can also just add barbecue or Buffalo sauce and serve on bread.

Chicken Salad	4 servings
1 C chicken half stalk chopped celery 2 T chopped onion ¼ - ½ C mayonnaise 2 chopped dill pickle slices small squeeze of lemon juice chopped nuts, optional craisins, optional dill s&p	Dice the chicken into very small pieces. Mix everything together. Fresh dill is nice to use, but dry will work. I like the craisins (dried cranberries) a lot, but have also added regular raisins.

Chicken Noodle Soup	4 servings
4 C broth 1 C pasta 1 C chicken celery carrots onion 1 t parsley 1 T dill 1 – 2 cloves garlic s&p	Chop and simmer the whole shebang until the pasta is done. Sometimes I use a lot of broth and/or water to make it really soupy, other times I use less. Also, when I don't have much or any chicken I just use a lot of veggies. The real key is the broth, if it isn't flavorful enough, add a bouillon cube.

Soy Stir Fry	4 servings
1 cup dry rice frozen stir fry vegetables 1 C chicken ⅓ cup soy sauce ⅓ cup pineapple ⅓ C pineapple juice ½ T - 1 T crushed red pepper 1 clove garlic ½ t ginger 1 T cornstarch mixed in about ⅓ C water	You can combine this in a couple of different ways, the easiest is to just throw everything but the rice in the pan, including the chicken (or steak or tofu if you prefer) and bring it to a boil. I think the veggies get overcooked this way and too much sauce evaporates. This is how I do it, put the chicken, sauce ingredients (except the cornstarch) and frozen veggies in the skillet, cover them with a lid smaller than the pan and let them steam for about 2 minutes then add the pineapple to the pan outside of the lid for another two - three minutes and then combine them, add the cornstarch that has been mixed with about 1/3 c water and bring it to a boil. Serve over cooked rice. It is pretty spicy if you use the 1 T of red pepper flakes. You can add more pineapple juice or use less pepper to adjust.

Chicken Curry with Rice	6 servings
4 chicken thighs 2T olive or vegetable oil, or butter 1 1/2c rice 3c boiling water 2 chicken bouillon cubes 2t curry powder 1t ginger 1/2t onion powder 2t salt	Preheat oven to 350°. Brown chicken in skillet with oil about 4 minutes on each side. Put other ingredients in large oven-safe dish and stir until bouillon is dissolved. Lay chicken on top. Cover with foil or oven-safe lid. Bake until rice is cooked (about 30 minutes, more for brown rice).

Potato Salsa Chicken	4-6 servings
3-4 large potatoes, sliced 1 onion, sliced 2T olive oil 12-16 oz cooked, diced chicken 1-2C salsa (or crushed tomatoes with salsa seasoning)	Put oil in large skillet or pot over medium-high heat. Layer onions and potatoes, sauté until browned (2-4 minutes), flip over, top with chicken, pour salsa over top. Cover and cook 5-7 minutes.

Chicken Pot Pie	6-8 servings
1-2lb chicken, cooked 12-16oz frozen mixed vegetables 2 chicken bouillon cubes 2C water 2T cornstarch 1 ½ t Jane's Krazy Salt 1T poultry seasoning Biscuit top: 2 C flour 1 T baking powder ½ t salt ½ C shortening 1 C milk (or water)	Preheat oven to 375°. Cook chicken and remove bones and skin (if applicable), then dice or shred meat. Combine all ingredients except biscuit mix and milk. Microwave on high or cook on stove until it reaches a boil (about 10 minutes), stirring occasionally. Boil 1 minute. Pour into 9x13 pan. Combine biscuit dry ingredients, cut in shortening (rub it between your fingers until the shortening is all mixed with the flour mixture) add milk (it will be sticky), press out on floured surface into a roughly 8 inch square, cut into 12 pieces and place on top of chicken mixture. Bake 25-30 minutes or until biscuits are golden brown. You could also use pie crust on top or top, bottom, and sides.

White Bean Chicken Chili	6-8 servings
1 pound dried beans, rinsed 1-2 lb chicken 1 T oil 1 T poultry seasoning ½ T Jane's Krazy or seasoning salt 1 t red pepper flakes 2 bouillon cubes 6 C water 2 C milk (or water), optional	Place the beans in a large bowl or pot and cover with water by 2 inches. Let soak for 8 hours or overnight. Drain and set aside. In a large pot, heat the oil. Brown chicken on all sides. Add the seasoning packet, beans, bouillon cubes, and water, stir well, and bring to a boil. Reduce the heat to medium-low and simmer, uncovered, stirring occasionally, until the beans are tender and starting to thicken, about 2 hours. (Should the beans become too thick and dry, add more water, about 1/4 cup at a time.) Remove from the heat, remove bones and skin from chicken if needed. With the back of a heavy spoon or potato masher, mash about 1/4 of the beans. Continue to cook until the beans are tender and creamy, 15 to 20 minutes. Add milk or water if a thinner consistency is desired.

Pasta

"Everything you see I owe to spaghetti."
~Sophia Loren

One Pot Pasta	6-8 servings
2 T olive or vegetable oil, or butter diced onion and/or peppers 12-16 oz pasta 4 C stock (or water and 2 bouillon cubes) 12-16 oz frozen California blend vegetables or whatever veg you prefer 1 portion seasoning blend (see below) optional – protein (cooked meat or beans) optional – 1 T cornstarch dissolved in ¼ C water	Cook onion with oil in bottom of large pot, about 3 minutes. Add bouillon, seasonings, and water to pot. Bring to a boil, add pasta, reduce heat to med-high. Cook 8 minutes, stirring frequently, then add vegetables. Bring back to a simmer, add optional protein, and cook for 3-4 minutes or until pasta is cooked and vegetables are hot. Tips: *If you have a lid available, keep it on as much as possible to keep the liquid from evaporating. *If all of the liquid has been absorbed and the pasta is not done, add about a cup more. *If the result is soupier than you like, add cornstarch and gently simmer until it thickens (about 2 minutes).

Pasta Variations/Seasoning Blends

Lemon Pepper	Curry Seasoning	Garlic and Herb/Italian Seasoning
zest and juice of one lemon 1T black pepper	2 t curry powder 1 t ginger ½ t onion powder 2 t salt	1 ½ t Italian herb mix 2 garlic cloves or ½ t garlic granules ¾ t pepper ½ t salt
Spicy/Mexican Seasoning ½ t cumin 1 t onion flakes 1 t crushed red pepper ½ t dried cilantro ¼ t garlic granules (or 1 garlic clove) ¼ t lime peel ½ t salt	**Basic Seasoning** 1 ½ t Jane's Krazy Salt 1 T poultry seasoning	**Vegetable Seasoning** 1T Dried bell peppers 1 clove garlic ½ T Italian herb mix ½ t sage ½ t onion powder ½ t celery seed 1 t Jane's Krazy salt

Basic Pasta Sauce

½ C olive oil 1 clove garlic, minced 2 t seasoning salt	Mix and use this on salad or pasta or pasta salad

Spaghetti Sauce/Marinara

½ medium onion, diced 1-2 bell peppers, diced 2T olive oil tomato sauce, canned diced tomatoes, canned crushed tomatoes, canned tomato paste, canned (only if it seems too thin) Italian herb mix garlic creole seasoning cayenne pepper (if you want it spicy) s&p pinch brown sugar (this cuts the kind of metallic taste tomatoes can get) canned mushrooms (optional, obviously, but makes it feel heartier without adding meat) red wine	Sauté onion and peppers in olive oil about 4 minutes over medium heat. Add other ingredients, simmer as long as you like. Spaghetti (or marinara) sauce is a little different every time. It can have really any combination and amount of the ingredients and will be delicious. If you want meat, add ground beef fried with onion, s&p and drained. Sometimes I add a can of Rotel, just for something a little different. The key is to let it simmer so the dried spices have time to re-hydrate and really blend. If you are in a hurry, you can eat it as soon as it's warm, but it will be better if you leave it on the stove on low (covered so it doesn't make a big mess) for at least a half hour or so. Serve over pasta. This sauce is also awesome to use to braise/slow cook beef or serve over meatball subs.

Vegetarian

The baby loves lentil loaf! Even if it, by all accounts, is one of the ugliest things I cook:

40

Lentil Loaf	6-8 servings
2C lentils 4 C broth (vegetable or chicken or water with bouillon) 2T olive oil 1/2C onion, diced 1/4C bell pepper 1/4C carrot 1/4C celery 2 eggs 1C bread crumbs 1C oats 1T Worcestershire 1 ½t Italian herb mix 2 garlic cloves or 1/2t garlic granules 3/4t pepper 1/2t salt	Bring broth to a boil, add lentils, reduce to simmer, cook 30 minutes (most of the liquid should be absorbed). Smash about half of the lentils with a potato masher or heavy spoon. In separate pan, sauté vegetables in oil until almost soft. Mix all ingredients together. Press into greased loaf pan (or any other pan). Bake at 375° for 30 minutes. Let sit for about 15 minutes before slicing. This is great as is, but I like to top it with a ketchup glaze (ketchup and brown sugar whisked together and microwaved until smooth) about 5 minutes before it is done cooking. I have also formed these into "meatballs" and pan fried them. If you do this it helps to smash most of the lentils and refrigerate the balls for a bit before frying.

Frittata	4-6 servings
8 eggs 2T milk 2T olive oil 1 clove garlic, pressed 1/8C bell peppers, diced 1/8C onions, diced 1/8C spinach, chopped Krazy Jane's optional: parmesan or feta	Sauté vegetables in oil over medium heat. Mix eggs and milk, pour over sautéing vegetables, cover. Cook until almost done, about 5 minutes (will continue to cook a bit after removing from heat). If you are using an oven safe skillet, then you can start it on the stove, then put it under the broiler to finish even more quickly and get a nice golden brown top.

Easy Vegetarian Chili	6-8 servings
1 medium onion, diced 2T olive oil 2 cloves garlic, pressed or chopped 2 cans chili beans 1 can diced tomatoes and green chilis (Rotel) 1 can crushed tomatoes 1 can kidney beans 1/2T ground cumin 1/2T chili powder 1/2T cayenne 1T seasoned salt or Jane's Krazy Salt	Sauté onion in oil over medium-high heat until translucent, add garlic and spices, sauté another minute. Add all other ingredients, reduce heat to medium-low. Simmer as long as you like.

Rice and Beans	8 servings
Beans ingredients: 1 pound dried beans, rinsed 3T oil, bacon grease, or butter ½ t cumin 1 t onion flakes 1 t crushed red pepper ½ t dried cilantro 1 garlic clove, minced ½ t salt 2 bouillon cubes 10c water Rice ingredients: 3c rice 6c water Dash salt	Place the beans in a large bowl or pot and cover with water by 2 inches. Let soak for 8 hours or overnight. Drain and set aside. In a large pot, heat the oil or fat. Add the seasonings, stir for 1 minute. Add the beans, bouillon cubes, and water, stir well, and bring to a boil. Reduce the heat to medium-low and simmer, uncovered, stirring occasionally, until the beans are tender and starting to thicken, about 2 hours. (Should the beans become too thick and dry, add more water, about 1/4 cup at a time.) Remove from the heat and with the back of a heavy spoon, mash about 1/4 of the beans against the side of the pot. Continue to cook until the beans are tender and creamy, 15 to 20 minutes. Bring water for rice to boil, add salt and rice. Cover the pot and turn the heat down to low. Don't take off the lid while the rice is cooking — this lets the steam out and affects the cooking time. Cook 18-25 minutes for white rice, 30-40 minutes for brown rice. Serve beans over rice.

Crock Pot Black Bean and Potato Soup	8 servings (pseudo-vegetarian)
Beans ingredients: 1 pound dried black beans, rinsed 3 T oil, bacon grease, or butter 1 slice bacon, diced (optional) 3 potatoes, diced 1 onion, diced 1 carrot, diced 1 stalk celery, diced 1 T Janes Krazy Salt ½ t smoked paprika 1 T red pepper flakes (optional) 2 chicken, beef, or vegetable bouillon cubes 8 oz tomato sauce 8 c water, chicken stock, or a combination optional toppings: bacon crumbles sour cream green onions	Place the beans in a large bowl or pot and cover with water by 2 inches. Let soak for 8 hours or overnight. Drain and refill pot with water to cover, cook 1 hour over medium heat. Drain. In a large skillet, heat the oil or fat. Fry bacon, if using. Add the vegetables, sauté until golden. Add the seasonings, stir for 1 minute. Put in crock pot. Add the beans, bouillon cubes, tomato sauce and liquid, stir well. Cook on low 6 -8 hours. With the back of a heavy spoon, mash about 1/4 of the beans against the side of the pot or use stick blender until desired consistency.

Beef and Other

Photo by Stephanie Scott-Huffman
Pre-Meatball above and Post-Meatball below

Meatballs

1 lb ground beef 1C bread crumbs 1 egg 1t Worcestershire or soy sauce 1T seasoned salt 1/4C finely diced onion	Mix all ingredients together. Form into about 25 - 1 inch balls. Bake or pan fry balls until cooked to desired doneness. Add to spaghetti sauce, serve on hoagies, toss in barbecue sauce, toss in jelly (really!), or whatever other application you like!

Campfire Beans	
ground beef bacon onion pork and beans dark red kidney beans, red beans, pinto beans, etc. 1/4 C sugar 1/4 C ketchup 1/4 C bbq sauce 1/4 C brown sugar 1 T Liquid Smoke 3 T vinegar 1 T salt and pepper 1/2 t chili powder 2 T mustard 2 T molasses	This is best made by first frying the beef, bacon, and onion then putting everything in the crock pot on low for 6 - 8 hours. We never seem to be able to wait that long/think that far in advance so we usually make it all in the frying pan. Also, as you might suspect, the amounts are very variable. I usually use 1/2 - 1 lb beef and about 3 or 4 slices of bacon and one can pork and beans plus about two other cans of beans. Also, sometimes I cut back on the sugar and/or up the chili powder to make a spicier version. My friend from ages ago, Kristen Burdette, passed this gem of a recipe to me during a playgroup when Levi was a preschooler.

Not Texan, but Really Good, Chili	6-8 servings
½ – 1 lb sausage ½ - 1 lb cubed or ground beef ½ cup onion 2T olive oil 2 cloves garlic ½ t crushed red pepper 1 t cumin 1 T chili powder 1 T season salt 14 oz can chili style beans 14 oz can kidney beans (drained) 10 oz can Rotel 28 oz can crushed tomatoes 14 oz can diced tomatoes ½ t brown sugar s&p	Chili follows the same rules as spaghetti sauce, anything goes, really. Fry the onions and meat until the meat is cooked through and the onions are a little translucent then add the garlic and seasonings, fry for just another minute (garlic burns quickly, be careful). Then add all the beans and tomatoes. I use whole cumin that I grind in a mortar and pestle. It tastes fresher, but can easily be substituted for ground if that's what you have. Cumin is what makes chili taste like chili, I think. You will have to play with the seasonings to get it just how you like it, I know we like it spicier than a lot of families. The amounts listed are just basic starting points. You can use just unseasoned canned or dried beans and skip the ones in the chili flavorings but it just gives you a little head start.
Taco Meat	If you remove the tomatoes and beans from the chili ingredients you get taco seasoning. Just add to ground beef (if you use the 80-90% lean you don't need to drain it). You can also add the seasonings to a can of refried or black or pinto beans.

Jambalaya

8-10 servings

8-12 medium shrimp, peeled and deveined 4-8oz chicken, cooked and diced 1-2 links Andouille sausage, sliced 1T Creole seasoning 2 tablespoons olive oil 1/4 C onion, chopped 1/4 C green bell pepper, chopped 1/4 C celery, chopped 1/4 C carrot, chopped 2T garlic, chopped 4 C chicken stock (or water and 2 bouillon cubes) 1 28 oz can diced tomatoes with juice 2 bay leaves 1t Worcestershire sauce 1-2C rice s&p	Sauté (on medium heat) sausage in large stock pot until browned and slightly crispy, remove from pot. Add olive oil, onion, bell pepper, carrot, celery, garlic and seasoning to pot. Sauté until onion and garlic start to brown. Add stock, scraping bottom of pot. Add canned tomatoes, bay leaves, and Worcestershire. Simmer on low for as long as you like. Increase heat to medium high and add white rice 30 minutes or brown rice 45 minutes before dinner is to be served. Add chicken, sausage, and shrimp 5 minutes before serving. S&P to taste. Remove bay leaves prior to serving. Options: If you like it spicier, add jalapenos, hot sauce, or more Creole seasoning Adjust thickness by adding broth, water, V8, or tomato juice You can add cubed white fish at end as well (or substitute the chicken or shrimp)

Stuffed Peppers	6 servings
bell peppers, any color or size 2 T olive oil s&p Filling: 1 ½ C spaghetti or marinara sauce ¾ C water 1 C brown rice ¼ - ½ lb ground beef or sausage 1 t seasoned salt ½ t Italian seasoning Optional toppings: fresh parsley cheese	This is such an easy recipe and a real crowd pleaser. I have it pictured as bite-sized appetizers, but we also love it stuffed in full size green bell peppers. If using the large peppers, we like to just cut off the tops, remove the seeds and stand them up in an 8" square pan so they hold each other up. Slice the peppers, drizzle with olive oil, sprinkle with salt and pepper, put under the broiler until they start to soften (3-4 minutes for small, 6-8 minutes for large). Brown the meat in a pot large enough to cook the rice in (I use the pressure cooker), add all of the filling ingredients and simmer, covered until rice is cooked (about 35 minutes on the stove, 18 minutes in the pressure cooker). Put filling in peppers and cook another 5-7 minutes under broiler or in oven. If you're a cheese loving family, at this point you could top with the cheese of your choice.

Salmon

"You piss me off you Salmon... You're too expensive in restaurants."
~Eddie Izzard (the rest of that bit is hilarious, you should look it up, it's not at all appropriate cookbook material, unfortunately)

Salmon is wonderful and healthy and also possibly the most over priced restaurant food. You can buy a 2 ½ pound frozen salmon filet for less than $10 (it goes on sale all the time), or pay $15 - $25 for a six or eight ounce piece in a restaurant. It's crazy. Plus, it is one of the fastest and easiest things we eat. It needs to be mostly thawed (but it doesn't have to be all the way), either by putting it in the fridge over night, defrosting in the microwave or putting it in the sink with cold water running over it.

Salmon	
Salmon filets Cajun seasoning	Sprinkle salmon with Cajun seasoning and put it skin side down under the broiler or in a skillet set to medium high heat. Salmon (and tuna) do not need to be cooked all the way through like most fish and if you do, they will be dry and ick. I like mine medium rare, but no more than medium. It should temp at about 135° which will look light pink on the outside and deeper pink and moist on the inside. If you cook it in a skillet, after about five minutes, carefully flip each piece. I don't like to eat the skin and the nice layer of fat (the healthy kind) makes it easy to slide the spatula between the skin and meat to flip or to flip it intact, then scrape the skin off. Then cook about another five minutes. Under the broiler do the same thing, but flip it with the skin left intact and then after the last five minutes, peel the skin off or just serve with the meat side up. Eating the skin is fine, I just don't like the texture, mostly (curiously enough, bears only eat the skin and fat layer and leave all the meat).

Salmon Nuggets with Spicy Aioli	
salmon filet, skinless 1 C flour 1 T Cajun seasoning oil Sriracha mayonnaise	Cut salmon into cubes, this is most easily done when the salmon is partially frozen. Heat about ¼" of oil in heavy skillet over medium heat. Mix flour and seasoning. Roll salmon in flour mixture. Pan fry in oil about 2 minutes per side, until light brown on each side (should still be dark pink in middle). Mix mayonnaise and Sriracha to taste and serve on the side.

Desserts

I want to have a good body, but not as much as I want dessert.
~Jason Love

Pie Crust	
2 C flour 1 t salt ⅔ C shortening 6 T ice cold water	Cut together flour, salt, shortening. Add water. Combine. Roll out on floured board. This makes two 9" crusts

Non-Dairy Pumpkin Pie (in case you want to bake for me)	
1 (9 inch) unbaked pie crust 1 (15 oz) can pumpkin 1 box cook and serve vanilla pudding 10 oz soymilk 2 eggs 2 t cinnamon ½ t ginger ¼ t cloves or ½ t nutmeg ½ t salt 2 T sugar	Preheat oven to 425°. Combine ingredients. (I usually add more of the spices than the recipe calls for) Pour into pie shell. Bake for 15 minutes. Reduce temperature to 350° and bake for 40 to 50 minutes or until knife inserted near center comes out clean. Cool on wire rack for 2 hours. Serve immediately or refrigerate

Muffins	
1 ½ C flour ½ C sugar 2 t baking powder ½ t salt 1 C milk or other liquid (a little less if your filler is really liquid-y) ¼ C oil 1 egg 1 ½ C filler spices (usually about 1 t, but adjust as you need to)	I love this recipe because it is a starting point for whatever we have. Just add 1 ½ cups total of any mixture of things, like shredded carrots or zucchini, or crushed pineapple, or chopped nuts, or chopped apples, or canned pumpkin, or chocolate chips or coconut, or... whatever! Just match the spices to what you add (or just go with cinnamon, it almost always works). If you want to go savory: crumbled bacon (pre cooked) and scrambled eggs (pre cooked) with sage, salt and pepper Mix all ingredients, place in greased muffin cups or whatever other pan you have (I like to make two shallow 8 inch squares). Bake about 20 minutes, depending on your pan size. They are done when a toothpick inserted in the middle comes out clean. Preheat oven to 400° Bake 18-22 minutes for regular muffins or 25-30 for large muffins.

Truffles

8 oz good chocolate, chopped finely ¼ C coconut milk fat ½-1 t flavoring (peppermint, orange, vanilla, coconut, whatever!) Toppings ideas: hot chocolate mix cocoa powder and powdered sugar shredded coconut crushed candy canes instant coffee	Melt chocolate in microwave for about 3 minutes on 30% power, stirring every 30 seconds. To collect the coconut milk, put the can in the refrigerator for several hours, then open the can from the bottom without shaking! You will be able to pour off the liquid and the solid part left is what you want. Mix everything together, put in refrigerator to cool. Scoop with spoons and roll in your hands to form balls, then roll in topping of your choice. I like about ½" balls.

Kara Cookies

Dry: 1 C oats 1 1/4 C ww flour 1 t soda 1/2 t salt 1 t cinnamon Wet: 1/2 C shortening 1 C brown sugar 1/2 C sugar 2 eggs 1 t vanilla optional: 1 C chocolate or other chips or chopped pecans	These are our go-to cookies but we usually don't put chocolate in them. We call them Kara cookies after my sister who likes the last cookies made from chocolate chip dough that don't have any chips in them. Preheat oven to 350°. Cream wet ingredients, add to dry ingredients, then add chips or nuts. Place about 1-2 T balls onto cookie sheets, bake 8-10 minutes. Makes about 2 dozen cookies. I usually make double or triple batches and shape it into logs and put it in the freezer so I can make a few cookies whenever the mood strikes (or, let's be honest, to just eat frozen).

Granola

½ C oil ¾ C sugars dash salt 3-4 C old fashioned rolled oats optional: cinnamon seeds nuts berries candy	Granola is VERY hard to mess up. I usually use a mixture of honey, white or brown sugar, and molasses, but whatever floats your boat works. Mix the oil and sugars in the microwave or on the stove until it gets all foamy, then add the rest of the ingredients. Spread it on a greased cookie sheet and bake at 250° for about 20 minutes, just until it starts to brown, then turn the oven off and leave the pan in it overnight or until it is completely cool, then break it into pieces and store in a closed container.

Chapter 8:

Non-Food Saving Tips: Where to Find Money!

There are a ton of blogs and books that will give you crazy, over the top ways to save money. I think there is a place for those, but it isn't necessarily to use those tips. Stay with me; have you ever learned a new word and then it seems like you hear it everywhere? That's how I feel about saving money, when I am thinking about it, when it is at the front of my mind, I notice tons of ways to save that are simple. A lot of the things I do started as ways to be a good steward of the environment, some things started as ways to save money, and some I do just because they make sense. The thing is that once you get into the habit, you forget why and just do. So, these are my easiest tips, but I'm sure you can find lots more that work in your life and I'm sure that some of these seem impossible, that's a-okay!

Tip Numero Uno - Use cloth.

Photo by Stephanie Scott-Huffman

We use toilet paper, but other than that, it is all cloth. It is so much easier to have a large stack of washcloths, towels, and napkins to use for all the goopy things. Trust your washing machine; cleaning is its whole job! We also have some really raggedy towels of various sizes that we use to clean things that are super dirty (remember, we have dogs and kids), then we just throw them away.

Cloth diapers should have their own chapter they are so great, but I'll sum it up as succinctly as possible. I spent between $200 and $300 to diaper three children. Total. It would have been less if I had known I would have the third and wouldn't have given away all my diapers. Plus, I used kind of "fancy" diaper covers on the last baby. Not to mention, nothing went in the landfill; I have a stash of the best cleaning towels you can buy; and all three babies potty trained at about 18 months, due in large part to the fact that they were more in tune with their bodily functions from birth.

I would think it would go without saying, but, of course, that means no paper plates, either.

Tip 2: Use less. Less what? Everything! Cut the amount of shampoo and conditioner you use; see what happens. Add a little water, see if you even notice. If your hair is still clean, cut back a little more until there is a difference. You will likely be surprised how much more than necessary you use. Same with toothpaste, soap, dish soap, laundry detergent, etc. It doesn't hurt to try to cut back, if there is a noticeable difference, then just go back to what you used before, no big deal. Another benefit is that it will require less water to rinse out all those suds, so you save water, too!

Tip 3: Pause and think before you hit the trash can, recycling bin, or garbage disposal. It is a great exercise to wait a second and make sure that you can't use whatever you've deemed worthless.

Examples:

Photo by Stephanie Scott-Huffman

*Zip top bags can be washed and reused. I'm not fanatical about this, if they have raw meat, something squishy, smelly, or otherwise icky, I toss them.
*Glass jars are definitely keepers, as are most plastic storage containers, if for nothing else, so that you can use them to send or take places that you don't want to worry about getting them back (food sent to new moms, grieving families, play dates, school functions, etc.).
*Plastic silverware, paper napkins, and condiment packs from take-out can all be saved and reused.
*If you have your children, particularly those who love crafts, almost everything is a treasure! Give an elementary aged kid an oatmeal container, toilet paper roll, the rubberband from broccoli, the junk mail, and some glue, scissors, and markers and you just bought at least an hour of free time!
*Do you remember the last time you used a phone book? No? What a shock! But they still bring you several every year, don't they? Use the pages in place of paper towels to drain bacon and fried things. You can also use them for lining the table when the kids are doing messy things; start your charcoal; make papier-mache; wrap presents, make seed-starter cups, and anything else you need paper for.

Look, another tip: Never buy anything new until you check the thrift store. You might be amazed at what you can find. I have a bit of a kitchen gadget addiction. If there's an infomercial, even better! The great thing is that most people buy those things, they sit unused for months, and then they donate them to the thrift store. I then pick said gadget up, also usually realize I didn't really need it and donate it back. The difference is that I paid 10% of the as-seen-on-tv price. Guilt free shopping! We are a tad clumsy here and break a lot of dishes, my favorite thrift store sells dishes and glasses for 10¢ -25¢ each. Sporting goods are another thing that are easy to find. Apparently, there are a lot of kids (and adults) out there who get brand new equipment for every sport they think about trying. I'm not saying do without something you want until it shows up at a thrift store, just swing by there first -see if you get lucky!

Making your own cleaning products can also be a way to save money and use fewer chemicals in the home. Make sure you price things out if your only goal is to save money, sometimes store brands or name brands with coupons (if you can remember to use them) are actually cheaper. I go back and forth in this area. I have to balance my "hippy" and "traditional" and "thrifty" personalities. I am willing to spend a little extra to buy healthier products, but not to buy name brand chemicals. Here is what I use most often:

Household Spray Cleaner	Seventh Generation (http://www.seventhgeneration.com/) or vinegar
Toilet Cleaner	Seventh Generation (http://www.seventhgeneration.com/) or bleach
Dish Soap*	Seventh Generation (http://www.seventhgeneration.com/) or Dr. Bronners (http://www.drbronner.com/)
Laundry Pre-Treater	Dawn dish soap (the original blue kind). Trust me, this is the only thing that gets restaurant laundry clean
Laundry Soap	the cheapest free and clear kind, sometimes mixed with homemade**
Dishwasher Detergent	the cheapest that includes enzymes, mixed with homemade^
Hand Soap*	Dr. Bronners (http://www.drbronner.com/)

*Buy a foaming soap dispenser and refill it with your own soap and water solution. You will use significantly less but still have plenty of suds.

** Homemade Laundry Soap
1 bar Fels-Naptha laundry soap, grated in the food processor
1 cup Borax
1 cup washing soda
Mix it together, then spin it again in the food processor until it is a fine powder or it won't dissolve in cold water. After you spin it, leave the lid on for at least ten minutes to let it settle. If you are using this by itself, then use 1-2 tablespoons per load (yes, really!) You can also mix this with boiling water and then use it as a liquid, ¼ - ½ cup per load.

I feel like I get better results when I use half commercial detergent, but then can cut the amount I use in half. Remember that we have dirtier clothes than most families, hubby spends a lot of time smearing fryer grease and black grill sludge onto his clothes (restaurant manager), the toddler leaves a fine layer of peanut butter on most everything, and I am super messy - most days I can't even identify the splotches on my clothes.

^ Homemade Dishwasher Detergent
2 cups Borax
2 cups washing soda
1 cup kosher salt
2-3 packets unsweetened lemonade drink mix (this adds citric acid which prevents a filmy build up and smells nice)

When I mix this about half and half with my commercial product, I can fill each dishwasher cup less than half full and still get great results (of course, I don't pre-rinse my dishes and it still works). If you use only the homemade, sometimes the results are less great and it also can get hard, but the commercial product has anti-clumping agents that keep that from happening.

One for the ladies: Two words – menstrual cup. There are several brands, you can find them online or at health food stores. It is a reusable cup that collects, rather than absorbs menstrual blood. You just empty and rinse it every four to twelve hours, depending on your flow. At the end of the month, just soak it in vinegar or bleach, or boil to clean for next month. They are fantastic! So comfortable and convenient, great for the environment, makes you more in tune with your cycle, plus, super cheap (about $30). What more could you want? I have used a Keeper and a Diva Cup and love them both. I lean toward liking the Diva better because it is silicon rather than the Keeper's latex which *could* in theory, possibly, under the right circumstances cause a latex allergy. Is it messy? A bit, but you wash your hands after using the bathroom anyway, right? Do not, I repeat do not get the disposable Instead brand cups. Conspiracy theory me thinks those were purely invented as a decoy to convince women that cups are too hard and messy to use. I tried them after many years of successful cup using and failed miserably, I'm certain a novice would end up crying.

Stupid tip: Don't go shopping. What? I know, right? If you don't go shopping you won't buy anything, pretty simple. I can't tell you how many times I have gone shopping because I was bored. Staying home or going to the park or visiting a friend are all more rewarding and free! Also, keep a running list of things you need so you can consolidate trips when you do need to buy things. How many people have the self-control to go to Target and only buy the toothpaste they need? Not very many! Even if you don't buy anything else on this trip, you will likely have seen something that plants a seed of desire. Something magical happens when you spend less time in stores, you start to want fewer things.

One more, tip: Give store brand everything a shot! At most, you're out a few bucks.

Like I said, there are tons of resources for frugal living, it is worth a little time to read more to get in the saving mindset.

Chapter 9:

Impress on a Dime

There are always going to be times when you need to impress someone – in-laws, parents, co-workers, birthday parties, etc. and the last thing you want is to look CHEAP! Here are my best tips and recipes to impress anyone with only a little effort and not much more money than you were going to spend on that meal anyway.

Tip 1: Think small!

Bite size appetizers and desserts are economical, easy to eat without utensils or plates, and make a lovely presentation. Plus, bonus – guests will eat less, but feel more full! It is an old dieting trick, small bites, eaten slowly, give your stomach more time to realize when you have had enough to eat.

Examples:

Photo by Stephanie Scott-Huffman

Bowl of hummus with crudités is nice BUT a platter of little peppers and pita chips with a teensy bit of piped hummus on each is delightful!

Pan of chocolate cake is delicious BUT tiny chocolate muffins with a dollop of whipped cream or icing and a chocolate shaving is divine!

Pizza if fine BUT pizza sauce, pepperoni, peppers, and onions rolled in bite-sized puff pastry is FANCY!

Seriously, everything is classier if you shrink it. Meatballs, truffles, cupcakes, cookies, sandwiches, you name it!

Tip 2: Ban the disposables!

Since you are already using cloth napkins and real plates in your everyday life, you wouldn't dream of using paper for a party, right?? Run to the Salvation Army (or your favorite thrift store) and buy all of the plates! Yes, you will need to wash them. The Earth will thank you and you will look elegant, fun, and whimsical, all for next to nothing. Salad size or smaller are best for large parties, no one wants to have to carry around a huge dinner plate.

While you are there, grab all the cloth napkins, too. Or grab a nice thick, 80%-100% cotton curtain or tablecloth and cut and sew your own napkins.

Tip 3: Puff Pastry

You can make your own, but I'll admit that it is tricky and frozen puff pastry is soooo easy, it is one packaged product I allow myself to splurge on. What do you do with it? Tons!

Photo by Stephanie Scott-Huffman

Roll out the pastry on a floured counter, spread it with an egg wash (half water, half egg, beaten together), put anything in it! Roll it up, brush off any extra flour, wrap it in plastic and put it in the freezer until it is firm enough to slice easily (or as long as you need to), pull it out, slice it very thinly, bake 425° for 10-15 minutes or until it is all golden.

Pizza and tapenade rolls

My favorite is the roll up – you can use pizza toppings; cheese and herbs; olive oil and herbs; cinnamon and sugar; olive tapenade; pesto; seriously, just about anything.

A close second is baked brie (also a super fancy, yet deceptively cheap option). Get a round of brie and slice the waxy coating off of each side (it's fine if some is left, it's totally edible). Sauté a rounded tablespoon of chopped pecans in a skillet with about a tablespoon of brown sugar and a pinch of salt over medium high heat for about 3-5 minutes, just until everything is melted and bubbly. Put the nut mixture in the middle of a piece of pastry and lay the brie on top. Fold the corners up and squish them together to make a little packet. Flip over, spray the top with oil (like Pam) and bake at 425° until it is golden, about 25 minutes. Serve with sliced apples and crackers. You can even do this as little minis! Divide the sheet of puff pastry into 18-24 rectangles, put a little slice of brie and a tiny bite of sugared nuts in the middle, fold and press the edges together and bake till golden.

Chapter 10:

Breastfeeding – Oh, What's Milk Got to Do, Got to Do with It?

Short answer? Everything. If you are concerned with saving, breastfeeding is for you. I'm only talking science and economics here, not judging or discussing the touchy-feely reasons, I promise.

*Breastfeeding is scientifically proven to reduce illnesses and death, even in modern, Western countries, including heart disease and cancer in the baby AND the mother.

*Breastfeeding is essentially free (moms usually eat a little more, but not a significant amount).

*Breastfeeding creates no landfill waste.

*Breastfeeding requires no bottles or mixing which saves time.

*Breastfeeding mothers employed outside of the home statistically take less time off work caring for sick children and, if supported by management, are more productive and loyal employees.

Kind of dry data to back up above statements:

Per the 2007 Agency for Healthcare Research and Quality (part of US Department of Health and Human Services), "a history of lactation was associated with a reduced risk of type 2 diabetes, breast, and ovarian cancer" for mothers. In addition, over the last 3 years, considerable evidence has accumulated showing that lactation also has important effects on maternal risk of hypertension, hyperlipidemia, and cardiovascular disease (PMID: 19110223; PMID: 19384111; PMID: 20027032; PMID: 20027032), the leading cause of death for US women.

****

If 90% of US families could comply with medical recommendations to breastfeed exclusively for 6 months, the United States would save $13 billion per year and prevent an excess 911 deaths, nearly all of which would be in infants ($10.5 billion and 741 deaths at 80% compliance).

CONCLUSIONS: Current US breastfeeding rates are suboptimal and result in significant excess costs and preventable infant deaths. Investment in strategies to promote longer breastfeeding duration and exclusivity may be cost-effective.

PEDIATRICS Vol. 125 No. 5 May 1, 2010

pp. e1048 -e1056

(doi: 10.1542/peds.2009-1616)

****

Cost of average powdered formula (Similac Advance $25 for 176 oz) for first year based on average feeding guides, no wasted formula, and no bottles.

0-3 weeks = 21 days x 21 oz/day = 441

3w-2mo = 35 day x 26.5 oz/day = 927.5

2mo-6mo = 126 days x 32 oz/day = 4032

6mo-9mo = 98 days x 28 oz/day = 2744

9mo-12mo = 84 days x 25 oz/day = 2100

Total = 10,244.5 oz = 59 containers = **$1475**

****

The cells, hormones, and antibodies in breast milk protect babies from illness. This protection is unique; formula cannot match the chemical makeup of human breast milk. In fact, among formula-fed babies, ear infections and diarrhea are more common. Formula-fed babies also have higher risks of:

Necrotizing enterocolitis, a disease that affects the gastrointestinal tract in preterm infants.

Lower respiratory infections

Asthma

Obesity

Type 2 diabetes

Some research shows that breastfeeding can also reduce the risk of Type 1 diabetes, childhood leukemia, and atopic dermatitis (a type of skin rash) in babies. Breastfeeding has also been shown to lower the risk of SIDS (sudden infant death syndrome).

Info from: US Office on Women's Health, Dept of HHS

****

Employers that provide lactation support experience an impressive return on investment, including lower health care costs, absenteeism, and turnover rates, and improved morale, job satisfaction, and productivity.

The retention rate for employees of companies with lactation support programs is 94%; the national average is 59%.

Info from: US Office on Women's Health, Dept of HHS

Chapter 11:

The Exciting Conclusion

The good news is that there really is no conclusion. As long as we are still kicking, we are still writing our story; and even when we are gone, the lessons we have taught will live on. Here's to making sure that your story is entertaining and delicious.

If you would like to get to know me a bit more, I would love to have you visit my, sometimes, but not often enough, updated blog at myfamilybz.blogspot.com.

I hope this book will help you feel more in control of your family's budget and helps you have a super day!

Index of Recipes

Asparagus, 31
Basic Yeast Bread, 32
   Cinnamon Rolls, 33
   Hummus Rolls, 33
Bean Dip, 30
Biscuits, 31
Black Bean Salsa, 30
Campfire Beans, 45
Chicken, 23, 34
   Chicken Curry, 36
   Chicken Noodle Soup, 35
   Chicken Pot Pie, 37
   Chicken Salad, 35
   Potato Salsa Chicken, 36
   Soy Stir Fry, 36
   Stock, 25
   White Bean Chicken Chili, 38
Chili, 45
Crock Pot Black Bean Soup, 43
Dishwasher Detergent, 53
Dressings, 34
   Honey Mustard, 34
   Oil and Vinegar, 34
   Ranch, 34
   Thousand Island, 34
Fried foods, 28
Fritatta, 41
Garlic Bread, 30
Granola, 50
Hummus, 30
Jambalaya, 46
Kara Cookies, 50
Laundry Soap, 53
Lentil Loaf, 41
Mashed or Cubed Potatoes, 29
Meatballs, 44
Muffins, 49
Pasta, 28, 38
   Basic Sauce, 39
   Spaghetti Sauce/Marinara, 39
Pie Crust, 49
Potato Chips, 29
Puff Pastry, 56
Pumpkin Pie, 49
Rice and Beans, 42
Salmon, 48
   Salmon Nuggets, 48
Seasoning Blends, 39
Steamed Vegetables, 30
Stuffed Peppers, 47
Taco Meat, 45
Tortillas, 31
Truffles, 50
Vegetarian Chili, 42

Made in the USA
Charleston, SC
02 December 2014